ORINSAY POEMS

THE WEIR OF ORINSAY

ORINSAY POEMS

A gathering of ten poems written by

MIKE BANNISTER

in the course of a quarter-century of happy times and adventures in and around Orinsay in the Isle of Lewis

'Is Treise Tuath na Tighearna'
(Gaelic proverb)

ORPHEAN PRESS

2012

First published in 2012 by Orphean Press
10 Heath Close, Polstead Heath, Colchester CO6 5BE

Typeset in eleven-on thirteen-point ITC Golden Cockerel,
printed and bound in Great Britain by Peter Newble:
10 Heath Close, Polstead Heath, Colchester CO6 5BE
peter@newble.com ❖ *http://www.newble.com/*

ISBN 978-1-908198-04-4

British Library Cataloguing in Publication Data
A catalogue record for this book is
available from the British Library.

Further copies of this book may be obtained from book-
shops, quoting the ISBN *above, or from Mike Bannister:*
Linthorpe House, 23 Station Road,
Halesworth, Suffolk IP19 8BZ

❖

Inscribed to
Kenny and Nelly Kennedy, and
to Anna-Marie and Murdo Kennedy of Orinsay,
with admiration and gratitude for all they have taught me
about Life, Work and Humanity, the Islands and the Sea,
and how it may sometimes befit the Poet
to laugh awhile at his own
solemn ways.

❖

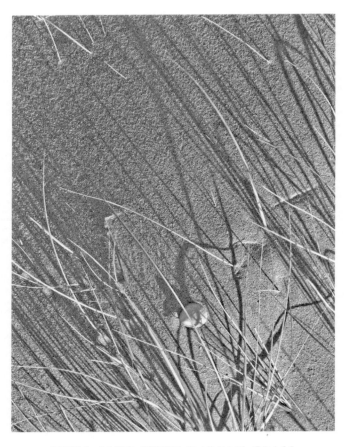

SHELL-SAND WITH MARRAM GRASS

CONTENTS

ACKNOWLEDGEMENTS

'Sound of Shiant', chosen by Edwin Brock for the Norwich Writers' Circle O. P. C. award, was later published, with an early version of 'Skiff Hallowing', in *Greenstreet Fragments* (Orphean Press, 2003).

'Strandloopers' first appeared in *Other Poetry* magazine, and later in *Pocahontas in Ludgate* (Arrowhead Press, 2007). 'The Weir of Orinsay' was first published in *Long Poem Magazine*.

SOUND OF SHIANT
Illumination

ONE said it was a change of air,
another felt the cold too great,
and the third stayed silent,
thinking perhaps the sea itself was dead,
with never a fish stirring,
under the sheer cliffs of Uisenis.

For sure, this was a small catch
after so many hours, lifting and falling
on the breast of the sea; and towards sunset,
with no more feeling in our fingers,
than in the folded iron of the anchor,
we turned north for Orasaigh,
thinking of homelights.

Yet ours, that night, would be
a different catch; a new thing to melt
the mask of tiredness, cold, and failure
from our eyes; from the shadowed wall
of Loch Sealg, the sun, dying in the north west
lit up the far shore, in a screen, gilded
and roseate, like silk or damask hangings
in some ancient court.

And framing this, as high rain
swept down toward Vaternish,
a great and merciful bow of light;
seven colours on seven colours
arched the full horizon, east to west.

Then, through that bridge of light
we saw aloft, two sea fowl,
white and brilliant, high-winging, slowly,
against the coming of the night.

STRANDLOOPERS
for J. M. S.

I
LITTORAL

SOMETHING about the unsettled merge
at the lip of the land, the restless shift of
water-light, the glancing energy, the faint chloric
'nose' of seepage and renewal is what matters
to us now. Ten thousand years, westering, we
traced the shoreline; the first true Pelagians,
winkling soft provender from sluiced cranny
and shoal; mollusc, cowrie, dulse and quick,
jointed, finny things, that are made and taste
of sea. The constant hunger driving us.

II
THE WEIR OF ORINSAY

THE clatter of his loom falls quiet. He stands
on the shore, stands a long time, leans on a forked
pole, his shadow turning behind him. He watches
the shingle break, like fish scales, glinting.
Under the steep ground, the slow tide filters
through a barrage of boulderstone and kelp. Low
water: a Black-back, and two smaller gulls come down,
eyeing the white sand, shellfish, urchins, corals, crabs;
of lythe-fish, saithe, eel, or sea trout: not a sign.
The weaver decides to leave them to it, this time.

III
AT HUISHINISH

A DIAMOND sky, and a savage wind cutting in
from St Kilda, drives shell-sand, jet-streaming
up the machair. We furl dry grass and heather,
into a narrow stone gully, roof it with splints
from a busted herring box and two beaten larch poles.
Third match, it smokes, then roars into fire. A feast
of easy pickings: fat cockles, blue mussels, dashed
through bright surf. In the bubbling skillet, they
gape on a bed of wild thyme and green wrack.
We are at home, on the far edge of the world.

IV
FROM ATLANTIS

THREE times this winter, they closed the wall
to turn a wrecking tide. Now, with the storm
gone down, I pick along the strand at Walberswick
with Jessie May. We find a tree that is both old and
young, thrown up from Atlantis. The pickled wood
is softish pine, its root, a leafy clutch of forest loam;
we finger it, hoping for some sign, a pupal case,
a carapace, a tool, an amber tear perhaps, left
petrified where the old Neanderthalers roamed,
before their world was swallowed by the sea.

3

THE SMALL HOUSE
AT HABOST

IN the small house at Habost,
it becomes possible to realise at last,
the Zen of nothingness, the essence
the beauty and truth of silence.

It slips into your life, discretely
at day break; following the soft tattoo
of gull-webs on the roof-slates.

This 'music of what does not happen'
is the interval in a curlew's song, out in
the mist, among the lily pools.

Or else, between the downbeats
of a raven's wing, sough . . . soughing
over, on a windless day.

Once, through these muffled larches,
as sunset burnished all the hills of Harris,
it seemed as if the silence whispered
in my ears, while night closed in.

THE PEARL
OF ORINSAY

OUT of the night she comes,
veiled among racing clouds,
a simple round of perfect light,
soft, and flawless among stars;
turning the wide sea silver.

Who sleeps and wakes again
far, far away, must feel content;
the self-same moon that lights
his longing dream, also lets fall
a light of pearl on Orinsay.

TALKING ORINSAY BLUES

pace *Woody Guthrie*

W ELL I packed my bag the other day
And wandered down to Orinsay,
And parked my car upon the quay
'n' gazed across the wide blue sea . . .
                              just wishing.

Then I put on my scarlet coat,
Joined Kenny in the Pea Green boat
'n' we headed out beyond Loch Seal
Hoping there to get the feel
                              Of real fishing.

Well all day long we hauled them lines
Watching the seagulls, seals and hinds,
And we hooked them fishes, one by one
Till Kenny squinted at the sun
                              'n' said 'Time to be goin'.

So we headed home upon the flood,
Hands all thick with guts 'n' blood
And in an hour we stepped ashore
With the biggest catch you ever saw,
                              Still wrigglin'.

We moored the boat and got the fish,
Feeling as good as we could wish;
Peeled our oilskins from our knees,
Saw a paper fluttering in the breeze,
                              just flapping.

There upon my car windscreen
In red ink like I'd never seen,
Was a bossy note addressed to me
From the 'Chair of the Grazing Com-mit-tee'
                              Some kind a warning . . .

6

'Cars', it said, 'upon this Quay,
Unsightly blue they'd tow away'.
Inferring, yes the pushy chap,
That mine was nothin' but a pile of scrap.
                              No kiddin'!

Now the way I see it this ain't fair,
I'll go and find this cheeky Chair
And see his nose above his chin
Before he turns my buggy in!
                              You see now.

Now there's a guy lives on the hill
Big 'M' they call him, I hear tell,
Ain't nothing happens in Orinsay
That he don't *authorise*,
                              I'm tellin'.

Upon his door I'll go and knock
'Call my new car an ancient crock ?
Are you the guy who laid that note
Upon my shinning mot-
                              -or car?'

Down Africa, I'll tell the tale
Of a secret place in a lonesome vale
Where elephants all go at last
When life and living's almost passed.
                              It's called a graveyard.

And then I'll draw attention clear
To the situation here,
And ask him why the hell he fusses,
This island's where they get to . . .
                              All them dead buses!

7

DUN BAN,
HER FORTRESS

Cromore, Lewis

BEYOND Cabharstagh*, the dream-road
falls away by fen and steep, until it
meets, almost, the tide of the salt sea;

there lies a silver lake, the shape
of a netted hare, that mirrors land and sea
night and day; and old men say

lythe-fish, salmon, char and mullet
swim together here, as if fresh water
and brine were one thing to them.

And at the collar of the hare, an isle
half-anchored to the shore by stone,
secludes the Corn-Queen's chambered

cell where, come winter's end, her king
entranced, and crowned with plaited gold,
in final consummation, comes to die

for sunlight on the furrow,
and the spring of the sown seed
at the heart of the heart of time.

* *say: 'Cavarshta'*

SKIFF HALLOWING

Port of Ness

For John Murdo Macleod,
Boat-Builder, of Stornoway

OF *Rionnag*, the charm of her building,
our son of the ninth wave remembers:

her levelled beam, the keelson tree,
The One securing, first to last,

raked stern and stem-posts rising,
Three in one; the horned keel,

Twelve strakes, his craft becomes;
land, board, and bevel meet cunningly,

clench-nails through the red grain;
form of a leaf, a tear, an open hand,

the first chrism, linseed and turpentine;
she rides; a gleam of honey in glint of sea.

God of the deeps from Barra to Cape Wrath
gift her with hopes of safe comings-home.

TO MARAG DHU,
A PRAISE POEM

for Andrew Howard of Forres, pace *Robert Burns*

MACLEOD'S dirigible, that recipe divine,
its hue so reminiscent of the Aubergine;
boiled, baked or fried, it has us slaverin,'
the 'Caviar o' Working Folk' nae bone nor gristle,
Oh! fry me a frizzlin' crust o' haemoglobin;
better than beef or lamb, and Scotch as thistle!

Encased with lard and salt and Barley seed,
the warm red humours of the hoggy breed,
are, in some vast *ballan*, gently poached,
then strung aloft to cure and take the air;
it only wants for pickles and warm bread
To mak' for us the noblest o' fare.

Then hail the sanguine hero, Charles Macleod
of Stornoway in Lewis, praise be heard
from Patagonia's windy plain to Gearraidh Bhaird*.
The best Black Pudding on the turning earth,
an epicurean wonder, we can all afford;
and simple nourishment of soarin' worth.

* say: 'Gary Vard'

THE GREAT BOAT
OF MEALASTA*

ALMOST a quarter-century has turned since we
first wondered at the sea-worn double-ender,
her ovine sweep of larch on oak, cross-planked
with elm-wood, ten foot in the beam,
scarred beauty, born from the seas' drift.

Now, there's only a knot or two of keelson beam
a sliver of garboard, pickled in sphagnum juice;
the rest is gone, wasted by time's gribble,
the worm, the wasp; its benches lifted, maybe
for the shuttering of some crofter's fank.

Across the strait, the isle is fallow green
since Southern rustlers, in sea mist, spirited
two hundred head away, and left a bobbing trail
of ale cans on the sea. For now, the grazing's
over; no one makes the crossing anymore.

That first day, a westerly fetching five
hundred mile, ripped at the coast, spume lifting,
way over. Now it is windless; out there, beyond
St Kilda, the zinc-grey ocean smooths to a bright
bevel of deep indigo. As the light falls

an unfamiliar sense, beyond the sadness
of an old boat dissolved in time; something
about these forgotten ways, touches deep
the two of us, together, a road without a name,
and one shared view of the far horizon.

say: 'Veo-loshta'

11

THE WEIR OF ORINSAY

I

A VIEW OF THE SHIANT ISLES

STAY with me now, at the edge of the world
a thousand mile from home, let go of time, this
warm September morning; there's a long bench
in the lee of the old Kennedy Croft, looking south
down the high-sided funnel of Loch Shell.

Silence like you've never known: a mirror turning
ice-blue, jade and white, a small sea with hidden
furies, an empty slipway, an anchorage of ghosts
where *Jessie* and *The Lark*, by net and line hauled
silver home, and somehow came to grief.

Nine mile out, from sixty fathom deep, the islands
loom, the foam-shot jaw of some leviathan, all dolerite
and olivine, a string of 'old men' like worn stumps, and
then, a jutting lip, that drinks an ocean twice a day and,
in accordance with the sun and moon, regurgitates.

Some call this archipelago The Enchanted Isles,
where Niamh of the yellow hair, stole Oisin out of
Ireland three hundred dreaming years; who's to say ?
Time, here, is not a matter for the clocks at all. Let us
be quiet together and feel the history of the place;

how the hard land was husbanded, then cleared
without mercy; and how the raider heroes won it back:
Kennedy, MacMillan, Nicolson, MacAskill, MacInnes,
fourteen houses, good roads and verges, planted now,
a loom, a cattle-grid, a post-box, lamp, and meeting hall.

Listen: it comes to life, birdsong, the amber tide,
a lamb, a song in the wire. The rifted cloud lets down
eight vast diagonals of light; a gold spider, compassing,
that weaves, un-weaves, and starts to weave again
the glory of this one September morning.

II

THE WEIR

EBB-TIDE island, a low green jewel
set in a north-cut fold of rock, a sheltering
for small boats, barring strong southerlies;

a place of particular qualities, ancient
retainer: an accidental pool, a navel in silt,
and boulders, a fish-trap, moon-worked.

I am drawn to its common wealth;
after a score of centuries, still it moves,
tides come and go, sometimes providing.

I'll try to learn the metre of it, acquire
a more even way of being. Time bids me
settle this account, to prize simplicities,

find some kind of gentleness, a longer
view, and the capacity, maybe, to give.

III

ON LOCH SHELL

AFTER so long in the foetid city,
I had forgotten how pure air carries
a sweet edge, here on the lifting tide,

how water splits turquoise and jade
from the sunlight's million guises; stirs
in me primordial feelings, finds new

degrees of wakefulness, the fore-edge,
the quickening, of possibilities and escape
from the long slow trance of dying.

I gaze far down, half mesmerised,
intent, thirsty almost for one brief gleam,
the lightning flicker of a swirling fin.

One hand on the gunwale the other
line-hauling in steady sweeps, tensed
for the snatch of a taken lure.

Reflections come and go, as falling
surf rolls cresting in under the stem,
to the ancient engine's *guff-guff-guff*.

Five mile out, the long Atlantic swell
lifts, and lets fall again our ancient craft;
we wait, and wait for the turn of the tide.

IV
TALES TOLD BY FIRELIGHT

THE slow *craic* always starts quietly,
a chorale, with recollections of the day,
findings, island lore, the links and ties,
and after, the little histories, one by one:

Do you remember, now, who was there?
when was that? the day, the year, the time

we fished close under the steep cliffs, six
hours, and brought home forty silver Lythe.

Another time, the old daddy seal trailed us
all day; and we caught no more than three.

How a fine blue lobster was found on
the door-latch; with bright sea-urchins.

Of the squall that caught us on the mooring;
and how the painter parted like a rifle shot.

How Rionnag *was almost lost, and saved*
from the Minch by the sharp-eyed weaver.

How six Kennedys went out to watch
The poet try his hand at cutting peats.

14

And 'The Grazing Committee' warned him
about parking his car on the jetty . . .

And the song that was sung about that.

How it snowed on a summers night,
and we were ferried home by car!

How Florence, at eighty, went by boat
to the lost village, and how she walked
three moorland miles home to Orinsay.

Starlight and storm; night has
hurried by, peat falls grey in hearth;
early hours, we seek our beds
and find the sun already rising.

V

RIONNAG AND THE OTTER KING

EIGHT years he keeps his distance, secretive
unseen, along the eastern grazings, holted away
in the clay caves and rain gullies by the shore.

Not so, this day of days, the skiff *Rionnag*'s
first floating; craned in slings from the jetty,
a swan in the morning sun, bright gold on blue
as we draw her alongside, step the mast,
bend sail and gear, then turn the diesel.

The bright twins of Aengus come down
in pretty hats and Sunday frocks, waving as we
put out between the skerries and the headland,
three mile into Orinsay, her summer place.

At anchor, she is safe and trim, new chain,
keel-ring to fore-deck and out through hawse
iron, deep into clear indigo three fathom;
wavelets chuckle along stem and strake,
she eases back in the sweet breeze, snubbing
gently, weightless, at ease in the bay.

We lie on the shore, unwilling to leave
just yet, prizing the first moment of being
mariners; then suddenly He's here, close in
minus all caution; a flurry, smooth head cocked
at the new arrival. He turns and dives for a
a second surfacing, now on the starboard
side, then vanishes, deep down and away.

No third chance, the only proof he came
lies in our joint witness; wonder above all
wonders, that he should trust us so, coming
near, from curiosity maybe, or with a *nose* for
the scent of fish-glue, linseed, turpentine.

It's hard to avoid a certain sense of kinship;
we of the salt tides, the four winds, admitted
to a wilder category of being, where even
the otter-king allows we co-exist, out here
on the edge, alive beyond all expectation.

VI

THE SWANS OF AENGUS

END of a long winter, we happen on them,
at first light; resting, they neither sing nor
preen on that dark lochan by the Tarbert
road, where Seaforth, vast fiord, surges
close in under the steep brow of Clisham.

Crowded on dark waters, a dream of
elegance, white, ice-white each high
raised head finished in a wedge ofgold
with soft black eyes. The bond-chain of
exile bears down, linking us, as wanderers
in the act of leaving the Long Island; they,
north, nine hundred mile, by wing, and
we for the same, south by road and sea.

This place is sheltered by small conifers,
a staging-post, with sweet under-grazing;
we catch our breath, and with no words,
at all, shift into gear, resume our flight.

VII

AT THE CAIRN OF GIEAROL

In May-time morning light, backs against
this shuffle of bearded stones, we settle, out
of breath, and view the township far below.

Somewhere a cuckoo calls against the bleat
of a lamb, a raven croak, a distant hammering,
and the thrum of a small boat coming in.

Smoke drifts from crofts one and three,
the washing blows at number nine, and at seven
the loom is clattering away; song of Orinsay.

We stretch out on the dry heather,
consider the fragrance of cotton grass,
shorn fescues, fern and cool Atlantic air.

Behind one bevelled slab's the honey jar
we stowed, years since, to chronicle our several
journeys here. On this long-standing mark

have boatmen, shepherds and hunters set
their sights, as we do, in these latter days to win
some slowness from the stream of time.

THE WILD GEESE

'In 1925 my father found the walls of the old house . . . he rebuilt, and covered it with heather, that's what everyone did in the end. I was fifteen or so then.' Murdo MacMillan: Nº 14 Croft

HE is over eighty now, strides out with me
to the gate where the metalled road begins,
his grey collie, close about my ankles. It is
a moonless night, soot-black. A south wind,

warm for late October, riffles the dry verge,
brings from the shore, that familiar chloric
scent of wrack and brine. Above us, the moss,
his flock hunkered, among the cuttings

strews of cotton-grass and rain-pools. His
drying peats, stacked like the cells of Skellig
Saints, protect his kitchen garden; its damp
loam leavened with kelp and shell-sand, and

meshed, deep, against master rabbit. More
than an hour by the glow of his fire we spent
sharing old stories, strong tea and pancakes;
before dawn, I must quit the Long Island.

As always, they have parcelled fresh eggs
for me to take nine hundred mile, the gold-gift
of an ancient lord. I latch the gate. He doesn't
turn. 'Listen' he says, and somewhere

high up, I catch a faint and ghostly belling,
far-off bugles in the dark, coming near,
then the whistling beat of many wings.
'Wild geese going over' and his old face

lights as if, somehow, an expectation is
confirmed, a guarantee, however small,
of time's follow, one season to another;
the sequence of his stars made evident.

OISIN WAKES

'Get up on the white horse,' said Niamh,
'and whatever happens, never dismount.'

HE had endured all the sadness
wanderers feel, being so long away;
the last fish in the Weir, detained by a
tangled sense of half-belonging.

Over the years, his friends grew
to be kinsfolk almost, their discourse
a slow rhyme of settlement, clearance,
exile, war and capital, the common stuff
that brings Community to life.

Then after certain tricks of time,
the land itself echoed with word
of his destiny; that those he loved
best would some day bring back his
gathered dust and float it there,
to come and go with each returning tide.

X
CODA: THE BALLAD OF CRAB CHOWDER

A rhyming Recipe for Murdo Kennedy, Navigator,
of Sunny Bank, Orinsay, Pairc, in the Isle of Lewis

LISTEN! And I'll sing to you a fable
of Orinsay's most famous life-boat master,
a foreign poet and a sea-food taster,
and how a mighty feast was brought to table.

There was a midnight rattle on the latch.
The door flew open and a nameless man
all wave-soaked, pale and tired and wan,
brought in the very finest of his catch;

Out of the sea, this gentle man has lifted
five crabs of garnet eye and massive claw—
enough to rip the hinge from any door!
We're humbled by the things he's gifted;

But there was something more to stir our wits;
six plump and silver Lythe-fish, panting, lay
their golden eyes all wide, they seem to say
'We're to be eaten by these greedy Brits!'

So History, once more, repeats her rhymes
and yet again, your strange '*non-domiciles*'
show interest in the treasure of the Isles
just as their fathers did, a thousand times.

But wait, this is the paradise of Pairc.
The spirit of the Isles is open-handed,
now that *les fruits de mer* are safely landed
we'll make a feast for Kings, before it's dark.

And so, three hours of time turn through the clock.
The kitchen fills with steam and briny smells;
heads, bones and shells are turned, as if by spells
intoa delicious, golden, gluey, stock.

Then master Greenstreet dices for an hour
meat, peppers, leek, tomato, onion, celery in wine
with garlic, fennel-seed and wild green thyme,
then thickens all with butter and potato flour.

He lets the oven, modest heat assume,
places the pot mid-way, and then he waits: until
the house and then the village seem to fill
with subtle, aromatic and marine perfumes.

Behold! Proclaim this! loud and ever louder!
We dedicate this un-fathomable tureen
to the Fisher King of Orinsay and his good Queen
'*A spicey Lythe-fish, and coral-pink Crab Chowder*'.

Sealbhaich, Dear Friends!—Enjoy!

NOTES ON THE POEMS

STRANDLOOPERS

Originally, a Pleistocene species of hominid, native to coastal South Africa subsisting on the sea. More lightly used these days to denote beach-combers, among whom so many poets are numbered. See Kenneth White: *At The Atlantic Edge* (Sandstone Press).

SKIFF HALLOWING

Son of the Ninth Wave*, John Murdo Macleod, Boat-Builder: On New Year's Day 1919, his father, John F. Macleod was aboard the H.M. Motor-Yacht *Iolaire*, when it foundered on hidden rocks in the dark, and began to sink. He secured a line from the sinking ship, and com-miting himself to the ninth wave, was dashed onto the shore; an act of bravery that saved some forty lives. Even so, more than two hundred souls, many return-ing home from the Great War, were drowned. Our J. M. M. was born in the autumn of that year.

in Celtic tradition, particularly Irish myth, the ninth wave is a symbolic boundary between this world and the Otherworld.

THE PEARL OF ORINSAY

This Poem was written to celebrate the Pearl Wedding of Nellie and Kenny Kennedy, August *xxiii* 2002.

TALKING ORINSAY BLUES

Dedicated to Murdo Kennedy, Crofter, Lobster-Creeler, Sole Owner and Proprietor of The Orinsay Bus Company—in the bad old days when it was con-sidered practical to leave derelict buses out in the sea air until they slowly, but surely, dissolved into the land-scape. This song was found on Murdo's windscreen, shortly after these events took place.

THE WEIR OF ORINSAY

Spread across the western seaboard of our islands from Iberia to Orkney, many small and remote 'townships' exist, some of them dating back more than six thousand years; locations that first attracted settlers to rock formations where wild fish, at certain states of the tide, might be entrapped.

In this sequence of just over two hundred and fifty lines, nine poems and their raucous *coda*, The Weir becomes a metaphor for the author's lingering attachment, stretching over five and twenty years, to the life of one such Hebridean community; its people, their ways of being, their stories and the extraordinary beauty and remoteness of the place itself.

Hopefully, the poem is far from being remote or inaccessible, indeed the *coda* is designed to act in the way that Ben Jonson would have his players 'trip their measure' at curtain's end, to bring the audience, all as one together. Yet the poem touches on deep questions of exile, belonging, and transience; whether (*pace* W. S. Graham and Basil Bunting) we come to possess or be possessed by the land. It alludes to the classic myths of Niamh, Oisin and Wandering Aengus which, in the time of The Sea Kingdoms, were doubtless common Bardic fare along these very sea roads.